Shibden Hall Halifax, West Yor

Welcome

Welcome to Shibden Hall. For 500 years, from 1420 to 1926, Shibden was a family estate, providing a home and income to those who lived here. Shibden Hall and Park still show elements of their former use. A significant number of records of the estate have survived, including accounts, wills, letters, diaries, plans and maps that date from the earliest days of Shibden through to the present day.

A number of important families closely associated with Halifax have called Shibden their home. From the first identified owner, William Otes in 1420, to John Lister who lived at the hall until it became a museum, each inhabitant has contributed to the story of Shibden and its continuing importance. Today, the house is a public museum giving visitors a glimpse through centuries of history reflected in its architecture and the collections on display. Shibden Hall is set within a public park and gardens.

Calderdale Museums 2019

The Otes Family

In the 15th century, the local countryside would have been more forested with fewer fields and stone walls. Sheep, after which the valley is named, were reared for their wool. The first person associated with Shibden was **William Otes**. He is recorded in the township of Southowram in 1399 and in March 1420/21 he was at his house at 'Schepdene', valley of the sheep. We assume it was this house, although there are two other Shibdens in this valley.

William Otes was a cloth merchant, who desired a modern house supported by its own farm. Exactly what the original house looked like is not certain, but the central H-plan of Shibden with half timbered gables either side was probably its extent. Situated conveniently between Leeds and Manchester, and next to Halifax, the principal town in the largest parish in the West Riding of Yorkshire, which already had a thriving trade in woollen cloth, essential to England's economic prosperity.

When William Otes was building Shibden Hall the principal materials available for building were stone, slate and oak. The design, for a late medieval house of some magnificence, was the popular H-plan, easily recognisable here: the two half-timbered gables crossed with the Hall. The lower walls are stone, with lath and plaster above, all resting under a weighty roof. The Hall is raised between four upright trusses or teazle posts. These are roughly cut oak trees placed upside down on blocks of stone or stylobats. The walls stretching between them have three horizontal members: the ground sill, the bressumer and the wall plate. These support timber laths or studding with plastered slate infills give the building its striped look.

William Otes' grandson ultimately inherited Shibden. This William married and had a daughter called Joan and, in 1456, with no other children and his wife now deceased, he left the estate to Joan in his will. Later, William remarried and had a son, Gilbert (1428-1508) and despite his father's will, Gilbert believed he should inherit Shibden as the eldest son. In the meantime, Joan had married Robert Savile, the second son of the Saviles of Elland Old Hall, a powerful family in the West Riding. Their wealth, position and determination to consolidate their land holdings, encouraged them to contest Gilbert Otes' claim. Between 1491 and 1504 the ownership of Shibden was in the hands of the court which finally decided in Joan and Robert Savile's favour. Gilbert Otes was awarded only a lifetime interest in the income of the property.

The Otes Coat of Arms.

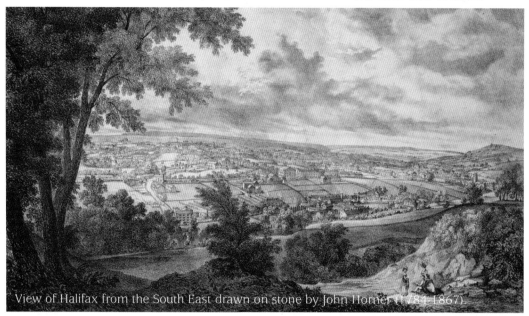

View of Halifax from the South East drawn on stone by John Horner (1784-1867).

The Savile Family

Joan and Robert Savile moved into Shibden in 1504 and redecorated the house and made alterations. The first major alterations to Shibden Hall were undertaken during the Savile family's ownership between 1504 and 1522. We believe that before then the Housebody was a double-storeyed room, lit by a wood mullioned window and heated by a central fire with a smoke hood rather than a chimney. It was narrower than today as the extension to the north came much later. Robert Savile extended the Housebody by about 3 feet (1 metre) on the south side, removing the existing wall, putting in a bigger wooden window and extending the windows above. He may have moved the fireplace to somewhere near its present position, installing a chimney and a fire window (to provide daylight within the huge fireplace), and he may also have floored across the Housebody, making two new rooms upstairs.

Such building archaeology is controversial. There are suggestions that there was once a canopy over a high table opposite the fireplace but the evidence is sparse. The new room, however, would have probably felt very confined and been quite gloomy, despite its polished panelling and gleaming metal. There was one door into it on the north side and another opposite to the parlours, but the location of the main staircase is uncertain.

The Savile Coat of Arms.

Joan and Robert's daughter **Sybil** was a considerable heiress from the Savile and Otes families. Sybil married **Robert Waterhouse (1498-1598)** and they inherited Shibden in 1522.

Painting of Shibden Hall by John Horner (1784-1867).

The Waterhouse Family

The Waterhouses were another established family and were bailiffs for the Priory of Lewes which owned Halifax. They collected the taxes due from the parish of Halifax and paid them to the monks of the priory in Sussex, about 300 miles away. Of course, over this distance, it was easy to manage affairs to one's own advantage, and the Waterhouse family probably did so. By just and unjust methods, the Waterhouses became more prosperous. There are records of an incident when the people of Halifax objected to the taxes.

It was not very long before the Waterhouse family rebuilt the south wall in stone with a magnificent 20 light, king mullioned window of decorative glass and drip-moulding above.

In 1545 Sybil and Robert's eldest son **John Waterhouse (1523-1583)** purchased the manor of Halifax-cum-Heptonstall, becoming Lord of the Manor, at the cost of £150 5s 10d. He married the heiress **Joan Bosville** and they had eleven children. **Robert (1544-1598)**, the eldest son, and David, the youngest son, studied at the Inns of Court and became barristers, while their brother Philip became a fellow of University College, Oxford.

When his father John died in 1583, Robert was resident at Shibden Hall with his wife **Jane Waterton** of Walton Hall, Wakefield, and their first two children. He was 39, with a busy professional life, and now also Lord of the Manor of

Halifax. His law practice in York was flourishing and he had property there.

In 1584 he was elected MP for Aldborough in North Yorkshire, and in 1589 served as Reader of the Inner Temple. This meant being in London where he had studied law, presiding over legal arguments and debates and acting as host to the many visitors to his Inn of Court. In memory of his father, Robert erected a fine tomb at Halifax Parish Church in a separate chapel. He then began extensive improvements to Shibden Hall, extending the house, redecorating and purchasing new furniture. In about 1585 Robert Waterhouse extended the back of the hall, providing the Hall with a dairy below ground, a new buttery and a new best chamber (now the Oak Room). Of their nine children, four sons and one daughter grew to adulthood. Living in York, the boys went to school to learn Latin, Greek, Ancient History, Religion and English. Their daughter Jane was educated by her aunt, Lady Gargrave of Nostell Priory, learning reading, writing, household management and needlework.

Robert was the respected head of the Waterhouse family, helping out with legal matters affecting his brothers and sisters, settling estates and negotiating for the family during the religious upheaval of Tudor times.

On his death in 1598, he left to his son **Edward Waterhouse (b.1581)** the property that he had significantly

The Waterhouse Coat of Arms.

enlarged, and entrusted to him the care of Jane, his mother, and his siblings.

Robert Waterhouse is buried at St. Michael's in the Belfry, the church alongside York Minster. Edward unfortunately did not fulfil his father's expectation. His wife, Abigail Barker, was blamed for encouraging her husband to neglect his duty to his father and leaving his brothers destitute of any friends. He was knighted in 1603, and in 1604-5 he mortgaged Shibden, two years later selling the Manor of Halifax. He did not resolve his financial difficulties and in 1612 he sold Shibden prior to being declared bankrupt in 1614.

Painting of Shibden Dale by John Horner (1784-1867).

Samuel Lister (1673-1702), artist unknown.

The Lister Family - 17th century

In the 17th century, Shibden Hall became the home of the Lister family, who would own the Hall for over 400 years, during which time the family's fortunes varied. It is from this period that most records of the estate survive, including the first inventory of contents of the house from 1677, and the first complete plan of the estate from 1791.

When Robert Waterhouse sold Shibden estate (comprising of the Hall, five other houses and 170 acres of land), it was purchased by a local woman, Jane Crowther, widow of Bryan Crowther of Halifax, who bought it on behalf of her nephew, John Hemingway for the sum of £1,600 in 1612.

Hemingway's uncle, **Samuel Lister (1570-1632)**, a cloth merchant, became the tenant at Shibden. The Lister family was already established in both Halifax and Hull. Samuel was married to Susan Drake and the couple had five children. Samuel was offered a knighthood in 1630, but along with many of his peers, declined the privilege, for which he had to pay a severe fine of £20.

In 1615, Jane Crowther and Hemingway's father both died. Still underage, John Hemingway was made a ward of the Crown and Samuel was appointed guardian to John and his four sisters, Sibil, Edith, Phoebe and Martha. John soon died, just eighteen months after his father, leaving the four girls as heirs aged just 11,9,6 and 4. Edith died just a year later in 1616.

Samuel decided to marry his sons to his nieces, who would bring to their marriages the ownership of Shibden Hall, adding prestige to the Lister family.

In 1619 his eldest son **Thomas Lister (1599-1677)** married his cousin Sibil Hemingway (1602-1633) and in 1625, his son John (1601-1662) married Phoebe Hemingway (1608-1695).

Thomas married twice more during his lifetime, to Phoebe Wood in 1634 after Sibil died and later to Mary Sutcliffe. From Shibden, he observed the upheaval of the English Civil War and fled to Manchester for a year with his second wife Phoebe and family. Before leaving, the family papers were buried in the gardens, to be disinterred somewhat damaged on their return. Thomas had at least five children and it is recorded in his brother John's pocketbook that the day after their father Samuel's death in 1632, with the house in uproar, his little girl choked to death on a lead bullet which she was playing with. She was buried in the same grave as her grandfather.

Thomas himself lived until he was nearly eighty, but had lost his sight during his last twelve years. He left Shibden to his son **Samuel Lister (1623-1694)**, with a record of all its contents in an inventory which was required to accompany his will. It records that Shibden was fully furnished with chairs and settles made comfortable with cushions, and with covers on the table. The meal arks were filled with grain; there was salted beef

and bacon in the flesh chamber and seventeen animals had been over-wintered. Thomas had a brass clock, a glass cabinet for drinking and eating vessels and a "seeing" glass. A small chair is also listed: we assume this is the oak child's chair bought for the birth of his grandson Thomas, in 1655.

Samuel married Hester Oates in 1651 and they had seven children, but no grandchildren. The eldest surviving son, also called **Samuel (1673-1702)** inherited Shibden in 1694, just six years before he died without issue. A portrait of him, shown opposite, is above the fireplace in the central housebody at Shibden.

The Hall then passed to the elder Samuel Lister's brother John's (1602-1662) grandson, who was **James (1673-1729)** and his wife **Mary Issot (d.1756)**. In 1702 the estate was greatly reduced in size, with James Lister inheriting the hall but only a quarter of the land. However, the younger Samuel's widow, Dorothy Priestley, had married Richard Sterne in 1703, uncle of Laurence Sterne (author of *Tristram Shandy*), but on his death claimed her right to live out her life at Shibden. She died in 1709.

The Lister Family - 18th century

James Lister (1673-1729) of Upper Brea, on the far side of the valley from Shibden, moved into Shibden with his wife Mary Issot in 1709. James also inherited his father's apothecary practice, with over 600 clients. The couple had twelve children; nine boys, two of whom died in infancy and three girls.

As a professional man, James Lister was relatively wealthy. The children were initially educated by Dame Gibson and later Dame Hopkins, the fees being 1s 6d per child per quarter. It was not long before the boys were sent away to school, first to Wakefield and then to Bradford Grammar, where the fees were 2 guineas a year.

John (1703-1759), the eldest son, attended St. John's College, Cambridge, where he read Divinity. He was there for seven years, taking a masters degree. The Reverend John's future was settled, initially as curate at Doncaster Church, then headmaster of Bury Grammar School. John retired from Bury Grammar School in 1749 and committed his energies to activities at Shibden. He was the first resident known to develop industrial interests on the estate. Shibden covered a rich seam of coal, clay and stone and he began coal mining and brick making businesses. New lead water mains were laid from existing wells to the house and 'Blind Jack' of Knaresborough was employed to build the road now known as Lister's Road.

Portraits of the Reverend John Lister hang at the foot of the main stairs and in the study.

James' sons Thomas (1708-1740) and William (1712-1743) were more adventurous and set out to establish trading links with the American colonies. Together they bought a share in a ship, a sloop called The Yorkshire Defiance. They were not particularly business-minded and aspirations to trade in wheat, pickled pork and rum were merely dreams. Deer skins, dispatched to England, arrived in unsaleable condition. Thomas, attempting to recoup losses, at one time bought and sold 15 slaves, a purchase which his brothers could not understand.

Reverend John Lister (1703 - 1759).

Reverend John Lister (1703 - 1759), by Richard Lynes..

James Lister (1705-1763).

Samuel Lister (1706 - 1766).

Thomas had married Anne Lewes almost as soon as he arrived in Virginia in 1733. William married her sister Susannah in 1738. He was a more conscientious man, moving to North Carolina and ultimately acquiring property there. Thomas died in 1740 after having a son, William (1734-1780), and three daughters, Martha, Mary and Susannah. William was lost at sea three years later in 1743, leaving two daughters. Records reveal Susannah's distress and later concerns about her financial situation showing how isolated the New World was.

John Lister's three daughters, Martha (1700-1789), Mary (1710-1786) and Phoebe (1717-1775) attended dame school, enjoyed the attention of the pastry master for 1s a week and received dancing lessons with Mr Smith. The three girls were expected to marry well, but Martha defied her parents by marrying William Fawcett of Halifax in 1722. The character of William Fawcett was accurately read by her parents and Martha was left alone at Shibden Hall with their baby William, who was to become General Sir William Fawcett K.C.B. (1727-1804). Mary married George Rose of Hampstead and Phoebe married a William Wilkinson of Hull.

The eldest son Reverend John Lister, who inherited Shibden, did not marry and died in a hunting accident in 1759. The ownership of Shibden passed in turn to his brothers, **James (1705-1763)**, then **Samuel (1706-1766)** who worked in the cloth trade, then **Jeremy (1713-1788)**. Another son, Japhet (1715-1782) was given Northgate House in Halifax and had two sons who died in infancy and a daughter Elizabeth. Portraits of James and Samuel hang in the dining room at Shibden.

James Lister (1748-1826),
posthumous, by Joshua Horner (1812-1881).

Anne Lister (1765-1836),
by Thomas Binns, commissioned in 1833.

The Lister Family

Jeremy (1713-1788) married **Anne Hall (d.1769)** of Butterworth End, Norland in 1744 and they inherited and moved into Shibden in 1764. It would be their children who inherited the Hall, not Thomas' who was in America. Thomas' descendants would ultimately inherit the house over a century later in 1855.

Jeremy and Anne had four sons and four daughters. Their second eldest son, **James (1748-1826)** lived to inherit Shibden after his father's death in 1788, living there with his sister **Anne (1765-1836)**.

Their brother Joseph (1750-1817) lived at Northgate House after marrying his cousin Elisabeth, daughter of his uncle Japhet who had married Elizabeth Wainhouse in 1747.

Their other brother Jeremy (1752-1836) was commissioned into the 10th Regiment of Foot (the Lincolnshire Regiment) on Christmas Day, 1770 and set out to join Colonel William Fawcett, a Lister relative. He set out for Canada and saw active service in the American War of Independence. At the Battle of Concord in 1775 he took a musket ball in the right elbow and was in Boston during the Siege. On his return to England, Jeremy was appointed Recruiting Officer at Gainsborough. Jeremy married Rebecca Battle of Welton Hall in 1788 and the couple had six children, four sons and two daughters.

When James died in 1826, he left Shibden divided between his sister Anne, his brother Jeremy, and his niece **Anne (1791-1840)**, who was 35 years old at the time and had been living with her Aunt and Uncle at Shibden since 1815.

Anne Lister (1791-1840)

Anne Lister (1791-1840) was the eldest surviving child of Jeremy Lister (1752-1836) and his wife Rebecca Battle (1770-1817). Returning to England from America, Jeremy had married Rebecca in 1788 and they settled on her estate at Market Weighton in the East Riding of Yorkshire. They were regular visitors to Halifax, and it was here that Anne was born on 3rd April 1791. Two of their sons died in infancy, a third died aged fourteen and the fourth, Samuel, died whilst serving with the Army in Ireland aged twenty in 1813. Rebecca died in 1817, the same month as Joseph Lister of Northgate.

Anne had already moved in with her Uncle James and Aunt Anne in 1815 and in 1826 when her Uncle died, she inherited a third of the estate, her Aunt and Father also receiving a third each, and seems to have taken over the running of Shibden Hall. Her father Jeremy and younger sister **Marian (1798-1882)** had also moved into Shibden by 1832. In 1836 Jeremy and Aunt Anne both died, leaving Anne to fully inherit the whole estate. Marian was bequeathed all their Father's possessions at the request of Anne.

Marian Lister c1855 (1798-1882).

Portrait of Anne Lister (1791-1840) by Joshua Horner (1812-1881).

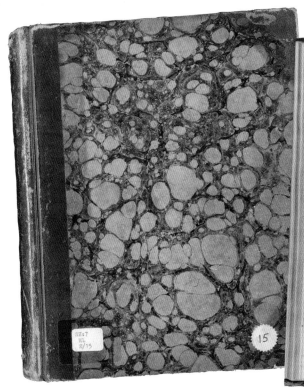

Anne Lister's diary from 1832.

Anne Lister was a diarist who recorded her life in great detail from 1806 to 1840 and the volumes of over five million words survive, along with hundreds of letters, account books and miscellaneous papers, all revealing a fascinating woman and life in the early 19th century.

Although never famous in her own time, Anne Lister's legacy has revealed her to be a remarkable scholar, traveller, businesswoman and property owner. Her diaries also reveal she was a lesbian and defied the norms of the time, not only in her relationships with other women, but also in how she dressed and conducted herself, resulting in her nickname, Gentleman Jack. Anne had a relationship with neighbouring landowner **Ann Walker (1803-1854)** who moved into Shibden with Anne and her family in 1834. The couple had a 'marriage' ceremony in York and in their eyes were husband and wife. Anne was an avid traveller and died in Georgia whilst travelling with Ann Walker in 1840.

Known locally as a landowner, businesswoman and member of the Halifax Literary and Philosophical Society, it was not until Anne's diaries were published by Helena Whitbread in 1988 that her intimate relationships with other women were revealed. Interest has increased steadily since then with a number of publications, ever increasing media coverage and the television series, *Gentleman Jack*, based on Anne Lister written by Sally Wainwright.

A separate introductory guide has been created about Anne Lister called *Anne Lister of Shibden Hall*.

Photograph of staircase in the housebody with the carved Lister Lion.

Anne Lister's changes to Shibden Hall

By 1836 the Lister family had been in residence for two hundred years. All around them, stone houses were being built by the wealthy yeoman clothiers, but the family seemed relatively happy with their home. Their principal architectural achievement was building the barn on the north side of the house. In the mid 17th century, the south front of the house was rendered and sash windows were installed.

It was left to Anne Lister to make significant alterations. At the beginning of the 19th century there was a trend for Medieval and Jacobean styles; Walter Scott's novels and Byron's poetry were best-sellers. Anne Lister travelled through England finding inspiration for her alterations in cathedrals, castles and ruined abbeys.

When, in 1836, she came into sole ownership, she selected the young architect John Harper to convert her dreams into reality.

The initial plans for Shibden were flights of fancy, the modest house flanked by castellated towers and halls on either side, but they were well beyond Anne Lister's means. Together they reworked the plans: the rendering was stripped off and the half timbering restored on the south front and new timber bay windows replaced the sash ones. On the west side a three storey Gothic tower would provide a library and modern water closets. By rebuilding the east side Anne created new kitchens and servants' quarters.

The crowning achievement would be to recreate the Housebody in an appropriate style. On 12 May 1836, Anne cleared out the upper rooms prior to taking out the floor and opening the Housebody to the rafters. A new fireplace was copied from the 17th century one at the Grange, a house near Shibden. Part of the buttery built by Robert Waterhouse was taken in for the staircase with the gallery above.

According to the bills itemising work by John Wolstenholme of York, forty two double twist balusters cost £29 8s; the fifty three plainer ones cost £6 12s 6d; the four figures in Norway oak cost a further £18 and Anne's family motto Justus Propositi Tenax (Just and true of purpose) cost £2 6s. Another significant project which Anne undertook was the cutting of cellars and tunnels under the house. This was part of a modern trend, ensuring that owners would not be disturbed by their servants.

When Anne left for Russia in 1839, work was continuing and John Wolstenholme was waiting for glass to be delivered from Sunderland to glaze the tower windows. Sadly, Anne died before the work was completed.

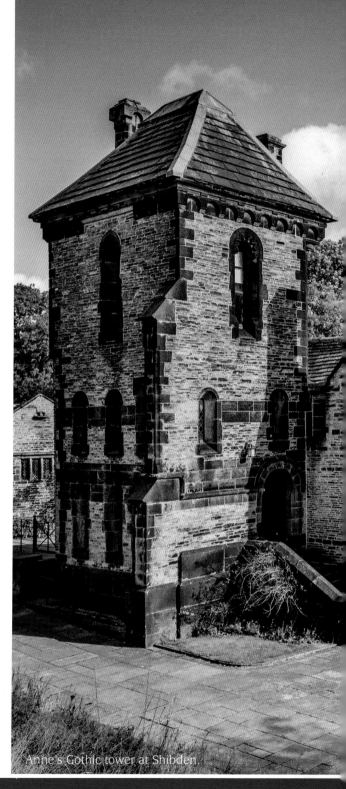
Anne's Gothic tower at Shibden.

Anne Lister's changes to Shibden Estate

Shibden's picturesque landscape was created for Anne Lister, who set aside 90 acres of the grounds in about 1836. Previously, this area was used for both farming and coal extraction.

The terrace was raised by John Harper to provide Shibden with an elevated platform. The house looks due south, and at the east end, Harper contrived tunnels for the gardeners to use so that they would not disturb the family enjoying the garden.

To the west is a series of terraces where an orchard has been re-planted with Yorkshire varieties of apple, pear and quince. The path passes the steps to the terrace, under some fine cut-leaf beech trees, to the 'Wilderness' that Anne created.

At the bottom of the track, the lake was part of Anne Lister's grand plan. The landscape gardener, Mr Grey, persuaded her to widen Red Beck, a small stream, to provide the impression of a larger river. The lake is dammed with an ornamental balustrade of sandstone, designed by John Harper, and had an added attraction for Anne when she realised she could harness the water power to run machinery in the wire works at Mytholm.

From the lake it is difficult to see the Hall on its terrace, screened by trees and seemingly high walls. Halfway between the lake and the Hall, there is a small group of trees, underplanted with daffodils. This marks the entrance to one of the old mines in the park, providing access to Halifax's notoriously shallow coal seams that were very difficult to work. A pit like this cost £2 6s 3d to sink in 1720, and a further 18 shillings to deepen it by four yards.

Anne Lister had a driveway built towards the main road to Leeds, now the A58, with a gatehouse supporting a Gothic arch at the end of it. She first used the road on 27 June 1837, when she drove to Halifax to hear Victoria proclaimed Queen. A few days later, when the gatehouse was finished, she celebrated by buying the masons a drink at the Stump Cross Inn.

Originally the estate was about 400 acres stretching from the Shibden Mill beyond Salterlee, down the valley, taking in the Hall and the Cunnery Wood above it on the hill. From there, the boundary followed the Wakefield Old Road to Mytholm. By Anne Lister's ownership, the size of the estate was much reduced. The remainder of the land, except the immediate parkland was sold in the 1920s.

Garden turret with door leading from the gardeners' tunnel.

Anne Lister's Gatehouse.

Dr John Lister and Louisa Grant

Under the terms of Anne's will, her partner Ann Walker inherited Shibden Hall. There are few records of this time, but it is known that Ann Walker was removed from Shibden Hall in 1843. Ann was taken to York Asylum and her brother-in-law moved into Shibden Hall. Ann never returned to Shibden and she died at her own property of Cliffe Hill in 1854. Marian long survived the others in her family and died in 1882, aged 84, but did not seem to ever reside again at Shibden.

Whilst Ann Walker was still alive several different families lived at Shibden. Anne Lister had mortgaged the estate in 1837 and to pay off the debt some of Shibden's contents, including Anne's library were sold in 1846 and some land was sold in 1847 for the new railway, which opened in 1850.

On Ann Walker's death the property reverted to Lister family ownership and the estate was inherited by **John Lister (1802-1867)**, the great-grandson of Anne's grandfather's brother Thomas Lister (1708-1740) of Virginia and his wife Anne Lewes. The couple had two daughters and a son William (1734-1780) who married Margaret Lewes in 1760 and they had nine children. Their son John (1771-1836) at some point returned to Swansea and with his wife Anne Morris (1780-1870) had a son, John and a daughter, Mary Ann. Their son John was a doctor by profession with a practice in Sandown on the Isle of Wight.

When they inherited, the family travelled between their two homes of Sandown and Shibden Hall. The account books reflect a man absorbed by Victorian science - he was a member of philosophical, palaeontological and microscopical societies.

John Lister moved in with his wife Louisa Anne Grant (1815-1892) and their two sons, John (1847-1933) and Charles (1848-1889) and daughter Anne (1852-1929) in 1855. Charles attended Cambridge University and was a qualified surgeon and travelled to Canada and the West Indies. He ended up in Santa Ana in Bolivia where he died and is buried.

Although Anne's building work was completed, the Hall and Estate needed much maintenance. The coal mines and the farm seem to have been profitable and further improvements were possible. The wages bill for servants for half a year at Shibden in June 1859 was £59 15s.

Dr John Lister, 1802-1867.

Louisa Anne Grant, 1815-1892.

An early photograph of the wilderness garden and cascade with young John and Charles Lister, c1860.

Dr John Lister's contribution to the alterations concentrated on the north front. He extended the present Dining Room - which entailed moving fireplaces and chimneys - and he re-timbered the exteriors of the gables. He also built the back porch with its Gothic motif and installed several fireplaces ornamented with simply carved tulips. Dr John's photographs of Shibden Hall, some of which are dated 1858, are a unique record of the house, alongside the earlier drawings of John Harper and Joshua Horner. Within the grounds John built the ornamental pond, around which he planted fashionable ferns and foliage. He also built a lean-to conservatory, called the Orchid House, and purchased a peacock for 15 shillings.

The eldest son **John** (1847-1933) inherited the Hall on his father's death in 1867. John was twenty years old and lived here with his mother Louisa and sister **Anne** (1852-1929).

John Lister and Anne Lister

John Lister (1847-1933) went to Winchester School, where a half year's fees were £26 17s 5d. From there he went to Brasenose College, Oxford, where he took his MA. By the time John Lister inherited from his father in 1867, Shibden Hall was no longer austere. The Housebody was cluttered with an amazing assortment of bric-à-brac including two organs, a telescope and a lionskin hearth rug. A new library had been accumulated, and John's mother had collected an assortment of domestic china and glass. John was extremely proud of his inheritance, showing people around Shibden and sharing its history.

John seemed content to live in the house just as he had inherited it from his father. Although he reinstated the decoration of the ceiling in the Savile Room, it was left to museum curators to investigate more of the secrets of the Hall. Amongst the architectural features that have been uncovered are the original fireplace in the Savile Room,

Keir Hardie (far right) outside Shibden Hall.

similar to the one above it in the Red Room. This discovery showed that the floor levels on the ground floor have been lowered by about 18 inches (40cm) from the level of the Buttery. Two of the original oak floors in the Red Room and the North Parlour Chamber were uncovered; revealing the 14-inch (36cm) boards, tongue and grooved as in a modern floor, but cut with hand tools.

John published extracts from his ancestor Anne Lister's (1791-1840) diaries in the local *Halifax Guardian* newspaper and his detailed research about Shibden and the town was published principally in the Halifax Antiquarian Society's journal, which John was founder president of from 1900-1933. He was also a member of the Yorkshire Archaeological Society for sixty-four years. Midway through life, he converted to Catholicism, much to his sister's disapproval. One of many tributes paid to John Lister was that he was 'kind to the poor'. He ensured there were soup kitchens arranged when the Pellon Silk Mill workers came out on strike. He was a founder of the Industrial School for errant children. He was governor of St. Joseph's Roman Catholic School and Hipperholme Grammar School, where he served for 47 years.

He stood as a Liberal councillor in Yorkshire and was a founder member of the Independent Labour Party. In the parliamentary by-election in 1893, he stood as the first Labour candidate for Halifax in a three-way contest, polling over 3,000 votes. In 1895 John, now treasurer of the party, underwrote the Independent Labour Party election campaign. Amongst political visitors to

John Lister (1847-1933).

Anne Lister (1852-1929).

Painting of Shibden Hall's Housebody, 1877 by Henry Sykes (1855-1921).

Shibden, John welcomed Keir Hardie, founder of the Independent Labour Party and (it is suggested) George Bernard Shaw.

After their mother died, Anne took over the management of the house, supported by a small and loyal staff headed by the cook, Mrs Kitchener. However, in 1923 when John Lister was 76, the bank called in the mortgages. It was a cruel blow. All John's money had been invested in charitable works and maintaining their home. John's friend, **Arthur Selby McCrea (1854-1945)**, a Halifax councillor, came to the rescue. He purchased the 90 acres of parkland originally created by Anne Lister which he presented to the people of east Halifax as a public park. The previously private haven of Shibden was opened to the people of Halifax by the Prince of Wales on the 15th October 1926, whom John Lister mistook for a newspaper reporter. McCrea also bought the reversion of Shibden Hall, which allowed John and his sister to live out their lives here.

Anne died in 1929 and John in 1933, when Shibden Hall was handed over to the Halifax Corporation.

Shibden Hall Museum

Shibden Park became known as 'The Happy Valley of Halifax'. It included a café, miniature railway and boating lake, which are all still present today.

After much discussion, the Halifax Corporation decided to open the Hall as a museum on the 4th June 1934. It was a remarkable task to sort out the accumulation of so many lives, the objects people held dear and the thousands of documents which contained their history.

Shibden's lake in the 1930s.

Left: the Prince of Wales planting a tree to commemorate the opening of Shibden Park to the public in 1926.

In October 1937 King George VI and Queen Elizabeth visited Shibden before heading to the Town Hall. It had been hoped to take the large dining table to the Town Hall, but it was too big to be removed so the King and Queen ate lunch at the table in the Housebody.

Private rest rooms had to be provided for each of the couple, so the Red Room was set aside for the King and the North Chamber for the Queen.

The Folk Life museum was opened in 1953 attached to the Hall. In recent years important restoration work has been carried out on Shibden Hall and the Park, ensuring that they can be enjoyed by future generations.

The King and Queen visit Shibden Hall in 1937.

Shibden's Owners and Key Residents

In addition to the list below, Shibden has been home to countless other servants and family members who have not always been recorded.

1420, **William Otes**

Unknown dates, **William Otes**

Unknown dates, **William Otes** and Margaret Waterhouse

1491-1504, Hands of the court

1504, **Joan Otes** and Robert Savile

1522, **Robert Waterhouse** (1498-1578) and Sybil Savile (d.1524)

1578, **John Waterhouse** (1523-1583) and Joan Bosville

1583, **Robert Waterhouse** (1544-1598) and Joan Waterton

1598, **Edward Waterhouse** (b.1581) and Abigail Parker

1612, Jane Crowther purchased for her nephew **John Hemingway** (Tenant) Samuel Lister (1570-1632) and Susan Drake

1632, Thomas Lister (1599-1677) and **Sibil Hemingway** (1602-1633)

1677, **Samuel Lister** (1623-1694) and Hester Oates (d.1692)

1694, **Samuel Lister** (1673-1702) and Dorothy Priestley (d.1709)

1709, **James Lister** (1673-1729) and Mary Issot (d.1756)

1729, **Reverend John Lister** (1703-1759)

1759, **James Lister** (1705-1763)

1763, **Samuel Lister** (1706-1766)

1766, **Jeremy Lister** (1713-1788) and Anne Hall (d.1769)

1788, **James Lister** (1748-1826) and his sister Anne Lister (1765-1836)

1826, **Anne Lister** (1765-1836), her brother **Jeremy Lister** (1752-1836) and niece **Anne Lister** (1791-1840). Her niece Marian Lister (1798-1882) later moved in

1836, **Anne Lister** (1791-1840) and Ann Walker (1803-1854)

1840, **Ann Walker** (1803-1854)

1843-1855 various tenants

1855, **Dr John Lister** (1802-1867) and Louisa Grant (1815-1892)

1867, **John Lister** (1847-1933) and sister Anne Lister (1852-1929)

1923, **Arthur Selby McCrea** (1854-1945) purchased Shibden, allowing John and Anne to reside there. He donated it to the Halifax Corporation

1926, **Halifax Corporation** opened the park to the public

1933, **Halifax Corporation** opened the Hall as a museum

The carved stone lion commissioned by Anne Lister in 1837

A Tour of Shibden Hall

The Kitchen

The Kitchen is dominated by the huge arched fireplace that was built in about 1560. Before that, this room was unheated and may have been used for food preparation, but cooking was either done in the Housebody (the main hall at the centre of the house) or in an extension, recorded in an exterior photograph taken in about 1860. By then this room had completely changed its use and was called the Morning Room. Anne Lister had installed new kitchens which are now used for education workshops and events, containing information on Shibden's history.

With the room reconstructed as a kitchen, you can see the two principal cooking methods prior to the installation of a range. Food was cooked in containers in a cauldron and meat was roasted on a clockwork driven spit.

Preserving food is essential. The 1677/78 inventory records £8 worth of salted beef and bacon in a "flesh chamber" and five meal arks (huge chests) of grain. The variety of brown, lead and salt glazed pots which were all locally made in Halifax and Bradford, represent some of the containers available for preserves, potted meat and butter.

The Cross Passage

From the Kitchen is the Cross Passage which connects the front and back doors and originally separated the service areas of the house from the living quarters. The polished panelling and candlelight indicated the wealth of the family who lived here. The oak settle dated 1711 is magnificently carved with a deep relief of flowers, semi-human forms, birds and an angel on the top.

The Study

Originally, access was directly from the present Kitchen, where it served as an unheated 'buttery'; a room for storing crockery. There was also a staircase to the upper floor, the remains of which are hidden behind the panelling on the far side of the fireplace.

The use of this room was probably changed by James Lister (1748-1826), who had fashionable large panels installed to cover the walls. In grander houses these were painted, but here they have been skimmed with lime and painted to resemble oak. The over mantel painting is contemporary with this eighteenth century decoration. The room is furnished as a study with an eighteenth century bureau and books from the sixteenth to the nineteenth century, many of them with Lister family signatures and name plates in them. On display are a barometer by Braithwaite of Halifax, firearms and a coaching whip and the portrait is of the Reverend John Lister (1703-1759) who inherited Shibden in 1729. The oak longcase clock is by Thomas Lister of Luddenden (1717-1779), no relation to the Shibden Listers.

The Housebody

Of all the rooms at Shibden, this has been altered the most. Its decoration today reflects the taste of Anne Lister (1791-1840) whose portrait attributed to Joshua Horner hangs above the doorway. As the central hall of Shibden, this room has always been the heart of the house where meals were eaten, visitors were received and business completed. The decoration reflects the prestige and status of the family through the ages. The principal pieces of furniture have almost always been here, but the decoration would only be familiar to more recent owners.

Anne Lister's work included opening the house to the roof; installing a new staircase and gallery; copying a 17th century fire surround for the fireplace and laying the parquet floor.

The splendid stone mullioned, 20 light window was installed in the 16th century by the Waterhouse family. The central armorial glasses record the previous owners of the house - the black cross and crosslets of Otes; the comical owls of the Saviles; the black reversed pyramid of the Waterhouses. The big armorial of Robert Waterhouse and his wife Jane Waterton was probably commissioned from the Huguenot refugee Bernardt Dinninckhoff in about 1585. All the other painted glasses are earlier than this and were acquired from churches that were being decommissioned by Henry VIII. Above the decorated window, you can see a wood mullioned window which lit the original upper storey rooms.

The wall opposite the fireplace is dominated by the portraits of 'Aunt' Anne Lister (1765-1836) by Thomas Binns, and Anne Lister (1791-1840), and James Lister (1748-1826) her uncle, by Joshua Horner (1812-1881). A portrait of the Reverend John Lister (1703-1759) hangs at the foot of the stairs. To the left of Aunt Anne, the teazle post has been boarded in, which is one of the principal upright supports of Shibden Hall.

Above the fireplace hang five portraits: Samuel Lister (1673-1702), Jonathan and Mrs Hall whom we think were relations of the Lister family, a portrait of a woman and a child, and Man with Rose. Hanging above the stairs is a view of the Shibden Valley by John Horner (1784-1867), commissioned by Anne Lister for for her sister, Marian.

The court cupboard seems to date from the 17th century but is actually a jigsaw of pieces of early furniture put together in the 19th century. This sort of cupboard was used for keeping linen, wine and wax candles under lock and key. The cupboard doors are decorated with intarsia work, which you can see on other furniture in the room. The floral decoration is made of inlays of fruitwoods and were originally brightly coloured. The long case clock was made by Thomas Ogden (1693-1769) of Halifax.

The staircase was designed by the architect, John Harper, for Anne Lister. Her initials are on either side of the gallery with the Lister family motto *Justus Propositi Tenax* - just and true of purpose - above. Here there is also a plaque recording the reversion of Shibden Hall to the people of Halifax in 1923. The Lister lion rears up as a newel post, holding the family coat of arms.

The fireplace is a copy of one at a nearby house, Shibden Grange. The brass fire dogs supporting the basket grate date from about 1690: they used to stand in the Oak Room in the Old Cock Hotel, Halifax: the room in which the Halifax Building Society was founded. They may have been purchased by the Savile family who owned the pub in the 17th century.

The large table in the Housebody was made in Yorkshire in about 1595 and brought to Shibden where it was assembled. Built of oak and made wholly with hand tools, the table extends on draw-leaves to about 16 feet (5 metres). It is suggested that originally there was only one decorative frieze rail, with the double C motif. The table would have been set on a dais with the owner of the house sitting centrally behind it and the family either side of them. But within fifty years the dais was removed, and the table set centrally so a carver was called in to carve the floral lunettes on the other side. In 1937 Halifax Corporation tried to move it to the Town Hall for the coronation visit, but it was too big to fit through the doors. In the end King George VI and Queen Elizabeth had to come to Shibden on their tour.

The bench alongside the table may also have always been at Shibden, while the settle dated 1690, like the court cupboard, has certainly been here since before 1845. The joint stools date from the 17th century - one is part of a pair of coffin stools on which the coffin was supported in the church. In times when status was declared by the chair one sat in, the master of the house aspired to a magnificent Yorkshire armchair like the one at the foot of the stairs, made principally of oak with high cresting and ears, and an intarsia back. Notice how the arms are not horizontal, but slope downwards providing a relaxed yet authoritative position. Such a chair would have had a soft cushion on it.

The Savile Room

This front parlour still recalls the ownership of the Savile family in the ceiling bosses carved in the 16th century when Robert Savile made alterations to the room in 1525. He added bosses to the new ceiling with an owl, initial 'I' for his wife, and Tudor roses.

The room was repanelled by Anne Lister in about 1834. She reduced a huge fireplace to make the room cosier and installed bigger windows. Anne Lister played the flute and piano and this piano is one of Shibden's many treasures. It is one of the earliest pianos in existence, dated 1769, and made by Johannes Pohlmann in London. He was a prolific maker of domestic instruments, yet few survive in original condition.

Chippendale style chairs provide comfortable seating. In the two cabinets are displays of ceramics: the blue and white earthenware are principally 18th century English tin glaze, a very fragile material imitating Chinese porcelain. In the regency style cupboard are pieces from Chelsea, Worcester, Wedgewood and Leeds factories. The longcase clock was made by Thomas Lister of Halifax (1745-1814).

The Dining Room

This was originally a bedroom and much smaller, with the outer wall being where the large beam can be seen, but it is recorded as housing two four-poster beds.

Today this room is set as a dining room and shows the new fashion in family dining habits after the restoration of the monarchy in 1660. The new king, Charles II, returned from the continent with several European dining habits which were slowly adopted in the provinces. Now the family would eat together, the servants dining elsewhere. Round tables which folded up were popular as they could be cleared out of the way.

Meals were laid out on the sideboard, higher than a table, on which there is also a square spice box. Spices were expensive and were kept locked up. Imported wines were taxed, so home-made wine or, more often, light ale was drunk.

In the Dining Room the chairs are all late 17th century in date, with high upright backs. The child's highchair on display was made in typical Yorkshire style and was listed on the 1677 inventory.

It is difficult for us to imagine our lives not being run by the clock, but before about 1650 households like Shibden would have been run without timepieces. The brass lantern clock was made around 1700 and is engraved Samuel Ogden (1669-1727). The livery cupboard dated 1681 is for storing food, with the initials of the owner on it.

Above the fireplace are the Lister coat of arms and the initials J. L. for Doctor John Lister who extended the room in 1885. The two portraits are of James Lister (1705-1767) and Samuel Lister (1706-1766).

One of Shibden's owners, Robert Waterhouse, left his initials above the wall painting in around 1590. It is now covered by the panelling in this room but can still be revealed by a room steward.

The Buttery

This room is one of the rooms built by Robert Waterhouse and closer inspection of the panelling and the joists suggests it was once two rooms. It is also suggested that Aunt Anne, who suffered from arthritis, used the room as a bed chamber, but her niece's alterations removed much of the evidence. In the mid-19th century it was opened up as a serving room for food brought from the kitchens through the door in the corner by the fireplace to the serving hatch. The longcase clock is by Thomas Lister (1717-1779) of Luddenden, the same maker as the one in the Study.

RW initials and wall paintings behind panelling.

Serving hatch to the Dining Room.

Close-up of the bench in the Buttery

The Oak Room

Upstairs, on the landing to the right, the door over the staircase leads into the Oak Room. Facing north, this room is always noticeably cold.

This was recorded as Robert Waterhouse's 'best chamber', built in the 1580s. The room was repanelled by Anne Lister in the 1830s.

The furnishing is from the beginning of the 19th century. The mahogany veneered longcase clock was made by S. S. Pinchin (1812-1872) of Greetland and plays six different tunes.

The North Chamber

At the end of the landing is the North Chamber. The edge of the walkway marks the panelled walls that Anne Lister installed to make this bedroom more private.

In the 1960s all the panelling was removed and the walls were revealed to show the rough original construction of Shibden Hall, and another of the early floors like that in the Red Room. The furniture dates from the late 17th century.

Along the walkway in this room is a glass door leading to the Tower, built by Anne Lister as the first stage in plans for a huge extension to the house, which never happened as she died before its completion. A spiral staircase leads up the Tower to a library at the top, used by later residents, but never seen by Anne as she set off on her last voyage before it was complete. A flushing toilet was also installed on the landing and the carpenter for the works was John

Wolstenholme, who followed Anne's specifications. The landing is home to a table and chair made for Doctor John Lister in about 1855 including a stag's head, part of the Lister crest.

The toilet for the Red Room next door now has a glass window so visitors can see inside and in the opposite corner is a door to another toilet.

The Red Room

This grand bedroom takes its name from the stencilled red frieze that goes all around the room. The wide oak floorboards make up one of Shibden's original floors. When the floor was laid, the wood was unseasoned or "green" and you can see it has distorted and cracked as the wood dried out. The boards are pegged together with 1 inch (25mm) dowels; each board measures over 16 inches (400mm) wide and 17 feet (over 5 metres) long.

The stone fireplace is similar to the one hidden behind panelling in the Savile Room below. During the Lister family ownership, the coats of arms of the Savile, Lister and Waterhouse families were painted on the overlintel. On the right, a little eight panelled door with its original hinges and latch opens to the Powder Closet. Originally this was the garderobe or toilet, the draught in which was so dreadful that Aunt Anne complained about it.

In the left corner is a doorway which used to open to the rooms above the Housebody. Anne Lister removed these rooms when she opened the Housebody to the roof.

The bed in the Red Room may always have been at Shibden, since it was made in about 1630. The headboard is richly carved with grotesque faces and includes two inlaid panels of intarsia work.

The Guest Bedroom

To the left at the top of the stairs, straight ahead
and up a few stairs is the Guest Bedroom. This
room was originally a storeroom, but in Anne
Lister's time was decorated with yards of fabric
hung like a tent and known as the 'tented
room'. With the great kitchen fire downstairs,
she described it as too warm for her to sleep in.

Porch Passage and Chamber

The passageway has some original floorboards and you can see the timber
construction of the Hall. On the wall is hung the funeral hatchment of Anne
Lister, which would have cost about £5 in the 1830s, and was hung outside
the house for a year after a person's death, before being removed to the
Parish Church. The last resident of Shibden, John Lister, rescued three Lister
hatchments from the church and returned them to Shibden, otherwise they
would probably have been destroyed.

The cupboards in the corridor originally housed Anne Lister's library, which
she had intended to be moved into the Tower, which she didn't live to see
completed, and following her death her library was sold off. Only a few books
remain in the Hall with her signature in them, displayed here with other
objects relating directly to Anne. The Porch Chamber at the end of the
corridor may have been used as a small study or dressing room and is where
Anne Lister's diaries were found.

Anne Lister's Bedroom

On your left are some very uneven steps leading to Anne Lister's bedroom. This room was later used by John Lister and none of the original furniture of Anne's time remains. The bed is a replica based on the *Gentleman Jack* TV series.

Very few of Anne Lister's personal possessions survive today. The few items of Anne's are displayed in the corridor, including Anne Lister's travel case, shown below. The red insert folds down to create a writing surface.

Shibden Hall's Archive

One of many things that makes Shibden unique is the size of its archival records and the information held within it, stored by West Yorkshire Archives Service at Halifax Central Library.

This is an extraordinary record with the earliest documents including handwritten indentures with wax seals dating from around 1400. There are several diaries, not only Anne Lister's, numerous letters from 1649 to 1933 and miscellaneous items including secret recipes and remedies, copies of poems, school books, share certificates, bills and sermons.

The Aisled Barn

The barn is over 300 years old and was first recorded in 1677. It is constructed with a Yorkshire slate roof, a timber frame and parts of dry-stone walls.

The fancy weathervane on the east end of the barn is a copy of one put up by the Rev. John Lister in 1749.

The cobbled floor has evidence of where the animal stalls were, and their hay would be stored at the far side of the barn up the steps. Some of the timbers have been re-used as they have several mortices cut into them which do not match the existing building.

Down a step in the corner of the barn is the Harness Room for storing, cleaning and mending saddles, tack and carriage equipment.

From the 1950s, the barn was used to house a number of historic carriages. Today there are five carriages on display, including the Lister family carriage, known as the 'Lister Chaise'.

The Lister Chaise

Built around 1725, this is one of the oldest surviving carriages in the world. It was used by the Lister family at Shibden Hall for many years and has the Lister coat of arms painted on each door. The green and gold appears to be the original colours, although at some point it was painted grey, before being restored and returned to its original colours in the 1950s.

It is a travelling carriage with broad windows, drawn by two horses driven by a rider, called a 'postilion', who sat on one of the horses.

The Carriages

The Park Drag

This carriage was originally a stagecoach and passengers would pay for a ticket to sit either inside or on top of the carriage. Drawn by four horses, it was built by Messrs. Holland & Holland of London between 1830 and 1840. It is upholstered in blue and there is also a toilet under one of the seats inside. It later became a 'drag', a privately-owned carriage. It could be used for days out with passengers riding inside, but able to sit out on the top in fine weather or for a good view. The crest may be that of Sir Christopher Furness (1852-1912), a businessman and Liberal Party politician who later became the 1st Baron Furness of Grantley, near Ripon in North Yorkshire.

The Park Drag.

The Post Chaise

Also known as a Posting Chariot, this carriage was made for Sir John Cowell-Stepney, 1st Baronet (1791-1877), a soldier, landowner and politician. It was used for travelling long distances and horses were replaced every ten miles or so at inns or 'posting-houses' along the route. The two horses were driven by a rider, called a 'postilion', who sat on one of the horses. Any servants would sit on the seat behind the carriage.

The Post Chaise.

The State Chariot

Last used by Sir Charles Hugh Lowther (1803-1894), this carriage was built by Holland & Holland of London in the 19th century. It was designed to display the owner's wealth and status and so was elaborately finished with windows that opened, fine carving, gold-plated fittings and the family coat of arms on each door. It was drawn by four horses and the driver sat on the high 'hammer-cloth' at the front, and two servants stood on the rear platform. A state chariot carried two passengers whilst a state coach would take four.

The State Chariot.

The Ambulance

This horse-drawn ambulance was built in 1912 by Wilson and Stockall of Bury, Lancashire. It was used in the Stainland and Old Lindley District of Halifax until the First World War. It has stretcher beds for two patients and a seat for an attendant. It also features rubber tyres and suspension to make it a more comfortable journey. During the First World War it was used to transport injured soldiers from Halifax railway station to several temporary hospitals in the area, as the main hospitals were filled up very quickly.

The Ambulance.

The Folk Museum

The Folk Museum was added to Shibden Hall in the 1950s to display a range of craft workshops reflecting the traditional way of life experienced by people living in the West Yorkshire Pennine area. In Sweden, folk life museums had already been established and were popular by this time, but in Britain their unique contribution was little recognised.

The Welsh Folk Museum at St. Fagan's was the first to be established in 1947 and the Museum of English Rural Life at Reading opening in 1951. The chance to break new ground in Yorkshire was made possible by the enthusiasm of the first curator, Frank Atkinson (1924-2014), who after completing the Folk Museum

at Shibden, went on to create Beamish, an open air museum in County Durham, telling the story of life in the North of England in the 1820s, 1900s and 1940s.

The workshops include a leather worker, basket maker, wheelwright, cooper and blacksmith. There is also a reconstructed brew house, pub, apothecary shop and estate worker's cottage, based on images from George Walker's *The Costume of Yorkshire* of about 1814.

Shibden is recorded as having its own brew house in 1677, but the one here today was recreated from 'The Old White Beare' at Norwood Green. The small pub is recreated from 'The Crispin Inn', which stood near Halifax Parish Church, now known as Halifax Minster.

The Saddlers.

The Apothecary.

The Estate Worker's Cottage.

Shibden on film

Wuthering Heights (1992)

Scenes were filmed at Shibden Hall for *Wuthering Heights,* directed by Peter Kosminsky, starring Juliette Binoche and Ralph Fiennes.

Anne Lister on film (1994 and 2010)

In 1994 Anne Lister's story was featured in the BBC Two series, *A Skirt Through Time* and in 2010 BBC Two broadcast *The Secret Diaries of Miss Lister*, a drama about Anne Lister starring Maxine Peake. Neither drama featured Shibden Hall itself.

To Walk Invisible (2016)

Shibden Hall was used for several locations for Sally Wainwright's historic drama, *To Walk Invisible* about the Brontës in 2016. The courtyard was used to replicate a coaching inn and the Buttery, Study and Savile Room in the Hall were all used to represent various drinking houses. Branwell Brontë was filmed in the recreated Crispin Inn in the Folk Museum and there was a scene in the Blacksmith's workshop, which was transformed into a stonemason's workshop.

To Walk Invisible ©BBC 2016.

Peterloo (2018)

The Estate Worker's Cottage in the Folk Museum also featured in Mike Leigh's film *Peterloo* about the Massacre that took place at St. Peter's Field, in Manchester in 1819, when cavalry charged into a crowd.

Documentaries

In 2010 there was a documentary produced about Anne Lister presented by Sue Perkins for BBC Two. Shibden Hall has since been used as a location for various documentaries on Anne, including an interview with Sally Wainwright for Sky Arts (2017), the BBC's *Antiques Roadtrip* (2018) and Channel Four's *Britain's Great Gay Buildings* (2018). Calderdale Museums interviewed Helena Whitbread in 2016 to create a documentary about Anne Lister which is shown on site.

To Walk Invisible ©BBC 2016.

Gentleman Jack ©Lookout Point 2019.

Gentleman Jack ©Lookout Point 2019.

Gentleman Jack (2019)

Award-winning writer Sally Wainwright came across Anne's story many years ago and always wanted to create a drama about her to share her story. Sally based the first series of *Gentleman Jack* in 1832 when Anne returns to Shibden after living in France and takes over the running of the estate. Whilst based on Anne's diaries and records of life in Halifax at the time, there are also several fictional elements, including the lives of other characters who lived on the estate.

After filming on site for *To Walk Invisible* Sally was keen to return and use as much of Shibden Hall for the locations for filming as possible. To facilitate this,

the Hall was closed to the public for several months during 2018, and scenes were filmed throughout the grounds, Hall and Barn.

As the furniture and Hall are Museum collections to be preserved for the future, much of the furniture and smaller items were temporarily removed from the Hall for safekeeping, and the production company brought in a great many props, including fake fireplaces, sinks and even a porch.

At the time of the TV series in 1832, many of the features of the Hall would not have been present, such as Anne's Gothic tower by the gate which was not completed until after she had set off travelling in 1839. The film company added a new porch, covered over the modern tarmac and iron railings with a

fake wall and added a dog kennel. The ornate gardens to the front of the Hall were added by a later resident so would not have been present in Anne Lister's time. The garden and grasslands near the Hall were left to grow wild for a few months so that during filming it looked unkempt, as it would have been when Anne returned to Shibden from her travels in 1832.

The courtyard features in a number of scenes with horses and carriages arriving with various guests and Lister family members. The original 17th century aisled barn was dressed to look as it may have done during Anne Lister's time at Shibden. Various animals were housed in the barn during filming, including horses, chickens, sheep and cows.

Halifax

Shibden Hall lies on the outskirts of Halifax, and although somewhat isolated from the town, the residents would have all had dealings in Halifax and attended churches, meetings, shops and business and visited friends and family nearby.

Halifax was historically a centre of woollen manufacture, culminating in the grand Piece Hall, opened in 1779 for the trade of pieces of cloth. The town's 19th century wealth came from the cotton, wool and carpet industries and like most other Yorkshire towns, it had a large number of weaving mills, many of which have been lost or converted to alternate use.

The Piece Hall.

Dean Clough, built in the 1840s to 1860s for Crossley's Carpets was one of the largest textile factories in the world at more than half a mile. Today it is a business and cultural venue. The Halifax Building Society was founded here in 1853 and is still headquartered in the town. Halifax was later known for Mackintosh's chocolate and toffee products, founded in 1890, including Quality Street, still made here today.

Halifax was notorious for its gibbet, an early form of guillotine used to execute criminals until 1650.

Halifax Town Hall opened in 1863, designed by Sir Charles Barry who designed the Houses of Parliament. The 15th century Halifax Parish Church became a Minster in 2009 and houses the Lister family crypt.

Halifax was also home to Lieutenant Colonel Edward Akroyd (1810–1887), a successful English textile manufacturer who created 'model' villages for his employees at Akroydon and Copley and was a great philanthropist. His home of Bankfield is now a public museum, managed by Calderdale Museums Service who also manage Shibden Hall. The local Duke of Wellington's Regiment (West Riding) have a museum within Bankfield and a chapel within Halifax Minster.

Halifax Minster.